W9-BEI-704

Table of Contents

What Are Parents?

Parents are people
who raise children.
Mothers and fathers
are parents.

Parents love, protect, teach, and play with their children.

Fathers

Fathers listen.

Matt tells his father

about baseball practice.

Fathers help.
Katie's father
helps her with homework
after school.

Fathers teach.
Mike's father teaches
him about flowers.

Mothers

Mothers protect.
Lexi's mother checks
her helmet before
she skateboards.

Mothers help.
Kyle and his mother
bake pizzas
on Saturday.

Mothers play.
Brenna and her mother
shoot hoops.

Glossary

family — a group of people related to one another

father — a male parent

mother — a female parent

parent — a mother or a father of one child or many children

practice — to repeat an action over and over in order to improve a skill

protect — to keep someone or something safe

A Family

Together, children
and parents are a family.